When I Go To Bed At Night

A Modern Tale of

Fear, Magic and Healing

Susan Bassett

Illustrated by

Ann Gates Fiser

Copyright 1994 by Susan C. Bassett
Illustrations by Ann Gates Fiser
All rights reserved

Library of Congress Catalog 94-071377-2
ISBN 1-885221-00-2

BookPartners, Inc.
P.O. Box 19732
Seattle, Washington 98109

Printed in Hong Kong

Dedication

*May this story of an inner journey give you the
strength and the courage to stand up to abuse and
shout your secrets to the world.*

This book is given in love to:

_____

Acknowledgements

*To all my friends and loved ones who gave me
unconditional support in my difficult journey
through the maze of truth.
And to my mother, and all my brothers and sisters,
including Henry, who is my inspiration, this book is
my gift of love.*

Susan Bassett

I'm not afraid of witches
Or dragons breathing fire,
And things most kids are scared of
I honestly admire.

I'm pretty brave
For a girl of two
With golden curls
And eyes of blue.

But when I go
To bed at night
That's when I feel
My deepest fright.

My mommy tucks me
Warm and snug;
We say our prayers,
Then kiss and hug.

Together we read
The fairy tales
About magic places
With nightingales.

But when she turns
Down the light,
The shadow appears
Later that night.

2

ometimes it's in the corner,
Sometimes it's by the door;
Sometimes it just stands there
In the middle of the floor.

Sometimes it sits right down;
Sometimes it walks around,
So quiet and so creepy
That it barely makes a sound.

Sometimes it's black as night,
And other times it's white;
But color makes no difference
When I see it in the night.

4

hen I was only two years old
The shadow came into my room,
And took me down the basement stairs
To a place of deepest gloom.

It laid me in the sawdust pile
And filled me with its rage;
That was the night I glimpsed the fairies
Dancing through the maze.

The sawdust chips were spun to gold
As my spirit leaped in fright;
A secret passage opened wide
In a flash of brilliant light.

Sparkle dust danced
Through the basement room
And marvelous rainbows
Lifted the gloom.

"Tiny fairies," I whispered,
"Hear my plea;
Won't you come now
And rescue me?"

Then, the frolicking fairies
Intent with their gaze,
Beckoned I follow
Them through the maze.

"Little Suzie," they said,
"Take our hands;
We'll lead you
To the magic lands."

Over valleys
In the sky,
The fairies taught me
How to fly.

On a carpet
In the air
Where I floated
Without a care.

I flew by castles
High up in the blue,
Where all of my dreams
Were sure to come true.

There were lots of children
Just like me,
Playing games;
I felt so free.

But when the shadow
Disappeared in the night
The fairies were gone
Out of sight.

And I was returned
To my little room
That had become
A place of gloom.

Oh, where, oh where
Can they be
Those little fairies
Who rescued me?

The fairies came
Until I grew,
Into a girl
They now called Sue.

15

hen I was barely twelve years old,
The shadow came again in rage,
Mother had a breakdown
And escaped her golden cage.

I was taken out of school
To tend my siblings needs;
And on that fearful night
I felt the shadow's final deed.

Do you wonder why
A girl of twelve
Would keep her secret
And never tell?

The shadow said,
In the basement cold,
The devil would get me
If ever I told.

My vision
Of leaping red hot flames
Bound me to the horror
Of those frightful games.

So, I ate the poisoned apple,
Drifting off to sleep;
Burying those memories
So very, very deep.

floated in a coma
Till years had passed me by,
When suddenly one morning
I awakened with a cry.

I visited all the houses
I lived in as a child;
I took pictures, made a scrap book,
Forced my memories to run wild.

The hidden thoughts kept coming;
The foundation soon was poured,
As I recalled the sights and sounds
And clanks of locking doors.

The pieces of the puzzle
Began to fit in perfect place;
I smelled the pungent alcohol,
I perceived the shadow's face.

Oh Daddy is it really you?
Would you have done this thing to me?
Could you really harm your little girl
And risk her sanity?

You broke my heart, I lost my soul
Which left me so confused;
How could I ever hope for love
When I had been so used?

21

Daddy please forgive me
For tears I cannot cry,
Although I see the anguish
Deep within your eyes.

I don't know how to love you,
I never will forget;
It's very hard to release the shame;
I haven't learned how yet.

My purpose now is healing;
That means that I must tell,
For if I keep these hidden truths,
I'll face your promised hell.

Hell is just a vision
Of my deepest inner soul,
To keep me trapped within myself
'Till I am gray and old.

I must fight to free myself
From my deepest pains within,
By looking at my darkest fears
I've held back from my kin.

y mother was a woman
Who always would abide;
Even when she disagreed
She stood by her husband's side.

She was meek and humble,
A servant to us all;
A loyal, loving woman
Who would save dad from a fall.

My mother said, "Oh Suzie,
I'm so sorry for your pain;
Your father's sick, can't help himself,
So you and I must pray.

"We'll ask God to forgive him,
We'll ask Him for his love,
Then Dad will surely find his place
In heaven high above.

"But you must keep your secret,
You must never breathe a word;
What would people think
If they ever heard?

"Your father is a businessman,
And shouldn't be disgraced;
He has a reputation,
You and I must save his face."

27

he priest said, "Just forget it!
Nothing should be told.
Keep your secrets to yourself,
And put your life on hold!

"What's the point in looking at
Memories from the past?
Your life is in the present,
Your depression will not last.

"Your father's old and feeble now
Not up to par at all;
Never, never again reveal
The nature of his fall."

28

ut what about my family?
Shouldn't they be told?
About my secret memories,
Of the basement dark and cold?

What if they have memories
Of the shadow in the night?
Holding back could harm their kids,
And keep them from the light.

We have an obligation;
It's our duty to unfold,
To educate our families,
The truth must all be told!

It's time to share my secret
With those closest to my heart,
My children and my siblings,
But I don't know where to start.

Will they think I'm crazy?
Will they think I'm dazed?
Will they believe my story
Of the fairies in the maze?

But the truth can be painful
As you will clearly see;
It's easier to deny the facts
Than face reality.

welve children in my family,
All out of control;
Which ones were abused?
Will we ever know?

My eldest brother Clinton said,
"I know our father well,
He'd never harm his children
'Cause then he'd go to hell.

"Dad often seemed so angry,
His eyes reflected hate,
But he cherished all his children;
His love for us was great."

Sister Elizabeth said, "You're crazy!
You've made this story up!
Anyone you tell
Will surely think you're nuts!

"Your visions are from the devil;
He works in the strangest ways,
And he will likely show himself
Within the next few days."

But with little sister Anne,
I heard her plaintive cries;
I also glimpsed the terror
Hiding deep within her eyes.

Her memories were vague,
Her perceptions so unclear;
The expression on her face
Mirrored my darkest fear.

33

Theresa has been shut away
Since she was in her teens;
'Cause all she ever did
Was let out bloody screams.

Her fear was of the shadow;
Her terror came at night;
A twisted, scattered child
Who refused to be all right.

The doctors say she's crazy;
She'll never be the same
Safely locked within her room,
And who's to take the blame?

I

t's time to regain the child in me
Who was stolen from the fold
By the shadow in the basement
Where the sawdust was spun to gold.

"I know your name,
The secret's out.
I demand the truth,"
I began to shout.

"Rumpelstiltskin,
Father dear,
That's who you've been
These many years."

ut that little old man,
Now feeble and gray,
Denied my truth
In the most fearful way.

He pushed me aside
And ran from my sight,
Shouting and screaming
With terror and fright.

"Your lies are from the devil
You must confess your sin;
No daughter of mine
Would slander her kin."

38

Then the shadow of the man
I feared most of my life
Suddenly disappeared,
Lifting the veil of fright.

It was broken and shattered,
Like a mirror in my mind,
No longer fearsome,
Unable to hurt or bind.

o take a healing journey
You must be willing to be strong,
To wield the sword of courage
Against someone who's done you wrong.

The freedom that awaits you
Is the truth that sets you free,
Which heals the inner child,
Releasing years of agony.

So, take that step to freedom;
Hold your head up high;
For you will free your spirit,
And spread your wings and fly.

40

41

The little girl named Suzie
Has recaptured her soul;
She's finally learned to love herself
And this has made her whole.

Transformation has unfolded,
Emerging from old wounds;
Colors of the rainbow
Released from the dark cocoon.

The butterfly of love
Has been unveiled for all to see;
A powerful and changing time
For truth and unity.